Words

to Live By:

Quotes

By

Shawntel D. Carey

2nd Edition

Words to Live By: Quotes by Shawntel D. Carey

Written by ShawntelD.Carey

Copyright © 2025 by SDC Compass Publishing LLC
All rights reserved.

SDC Compass Publishing LLC
sdccompasspublishingllc@gmail.com

Book Cover, Interior and Layout Design by Shawntel D. Carey

2nd Edition 2025

Printed in the United States of America

ISBN: 979-8-9939033-3-0

DEDICATION

To my late great-grandmother, whose strength shaped generations and whose light continues to guide my steps. You are profoundly missed.

To my cousin, the late Minister Jennifer Sorrell, whose grace, and kindness remain a lasting testament to the life you lived.

ACKNOWLEDGEMENTS

To my daughter, Mackenzie Mae, You are loved beyond measure. The depth of my gratitude for you is immeasurable.

My sincerest appreciation goes to Mrs. Catherine Jones and the late Mr. Emile Jones, Jr. Your kindness, generosity, and steadfast example of love have shaped my life in countless ways.

A heartfelt thank you to my dear friend, Janeen Sizemore. Your support and encouragement during the release of the first edition is something that I remain deeply grateful for.

To my family and friends, especially those in the San Francisco Bay Area, thank you for grounding me, loving me, and helping me become the woman I am today. Thank you all. I love you dearly.

TABLE OF CONTENTS

Character & Integrity 1

Grit, Grace & Growth 12

The Scholar Within 25

Love, Truth & Accountability 41

Restoration & Resilience 54

Becoming Your Highest Self 68

Citizenship & Responsibility 82

Principles to Live By... 92

INTRODUCTION

This second edition represents a refined and more intentional expression of my work. When I first published Words to Live By in 2022, it reflected my thoughts and experiences during a significant period of my life. As time passed, I realized that the original version, while meaningful, deserved a presentation that fully honored the depth of the work and the personal evolution behind it.

In this updated edition, the design, structure, and details have been elevated to match the clarity, growth, and maturity that have unfolded in my own life. Some imperfections have been corrected, and the layout now better reflects the tone and purpose of the messages. My hope is that this edition offers a smoother, more impactful reading experience while staying true to the authenticity of the original work. Thank you for returning to this journey with me or for beginning it for the first time. I am grateful.

ABOUT THE AUTHOR

Shawntel D. Carey, MPA, is an accomplished entrepreneur, author, publisher, and public servant dedicated to fostering clarity, purpose, and personal growth. A native of the San Francisco Bay Area, now residing in the metro Atlanta area, she approaches her work with integrity, discipline, and an unwavering commitment to excellence. Her writing inspires readers to think boldly, live authentically, and remain anchored in the values that shape a meaningful life.

─── ✦ ───

Character & Integrity

─── ✦ ───

What people do when no one is
looking is actually their truth.
Action tells you more than words ever will.

-Shawntel D. Carey, 2021

Class and Decency.
Please do not forget that
this is what we stand for!

-Shawntel D. Carey, 2019

Asinine!
Never be the reason for the reference.

-Shawntel D. Carey, 2019

Don't make assumptions about people.
Everyone has something about themselves
that is absolutely wonderful.

-Shawntel D. Carey, 2022

Without respect, nothing else matters.

-Shawntel D. Carey, 2021

Yesterday, today, and tomorrow,
we shall undoubtedly be held in high regard
because of our solid character

-Shawntel D. Carey, 2021

We can only really hope to be decent, well-raised adults with nothing but good intentions for other human beings.

-Shawntel D. Carey, 2021

A great hope is to never burn bridges,
if it can be avoided; however, kindly, and quietly
remove yourself when regarded as optional.
Allow the confused to dwell in their bewilderment.

-Shawntel D. Carey, 2025

Be thankful more often than not.
Situations in life will humble you.
Be grateful each and every day.

-Shawntel D. Carey, 2019

I loathe thieves.
Do not infringe on anyone else's intellectual property.
Don't be a thief!
Be original.
It's worth more.

-Shawntel D. Carey, 2017

——— ✦ ———

Grit, Grace & Growth

——— ✦ ———

Life is not going to be easy.
So, what!
Just maintain respect for yourself.

-Shawntel D. Carey, 2022

As a reminder to those who are at the beginning stages of a pursuit, never give up! It won't be easy. Use your grit, consistency, focus, and dedication to prevail.

-Shawntel D. Carey, 2021

Simply just stop choosing things
that are not in your best interest.

-Shawntel D. Carey, 2020

Feel the pain of discipline
or the pain of regret. It's your choice!
Discipline is self-love.

-Shawntel D. Carey, 2020

Consistency...
is the moral of the story.

-Shawntel D. Carey, 2020

Give yourself time to adjust while
being eager to find out what comes next.

-Shawntel D. Carey, 2011

The appropriate actions will follow
once you have made up your mind
and have committed to the process.
Define your process in five steps or less.
You got this!

-Shawntel D. Carey, 2019

Newly acquired success must not go to our heads.
I am glad that I once had it all and lost it all.
Rebuilding is now based on the number
of lives that can be impacted and elevated.

-Shawntel D. Carey, 2019

Shawntel D. Carey

It's Grind Time.
Hustle.
Now Hustle Harder!

-Shawntel D. Carey, 2021

I urge you to welcome the challenge!

-Shawntel D. Carey, 2022

Stay Focused.

-Shawntel D. Carey, 2019

Never underestimate the
message because of the messenger.
Be grateful, have faith, and take heed.
It takes grit and grace. Now, carry on.

-Shawntel D. Carey, 2019

The Scholar Within

Read, Write, Think and Act.
The choice belongs to you but,
the equation (R/W)T=A does not change.

-Shawntel D. Carey, 2021

Read to write well, write to speak well,
read and write well to think deeply,
think deeply and act accordingly.

-Shawntel D. Carey, 2018

Reading and writing are fundamental
in the pursuit of having a faculty that
does not allow for gullibility.

-Shawntel D. Carey, 2021

In no way am I credulous.
However, I am always willing to learn, seeking to
uncover the empirical value in all that is consumed.

-Shawntel D. Carey, 2021

Value education.
Develop a network within a community that
values and supports education as well.

-Shawntel D. Carey, 2021

Education is key.
Knowledge can never be taken from you.
Seek it, obtain it, and be it!

-Shawntel D. Carey, 2011

Love to learn,
then to be tested in order to
gauge your level of understanding.

-Shawntel D. Carey, 2017

Replace all negative thoughts
with thoughts and actions
that are positively positive!

-Shawntel D. Carey, 2022

The existence of plans, baselines, and formulas is an indication that you are meeting and achieving your goals.

-Shawntel D. Carey, 2019

Know your purpose.
Set out to reach your maximum potential but do so
with the objective of being in service to others.

-Shawntel D. Carey, 2020

To all of the individuals that have conquered an educational goal under extraordinary circumstances, especially single parents that have pushed through devastation to arrive at success; You are my hero!

-Shawntel D. Carey, 2018

Ask me if I want to hang out.
The answer is yes! But I can't;
I must study in order to get these degrees.
Rain check, please!

-Shawntel D. Carey, 2021

Share your knowledge
along the way.

-Shawntel D. Carey, 2018

Mentorship is important.
In fact, the best thanks, I've ever received was
"Thank you for mentoring me."

-Shawntel D. Carey, 2019

Common sense is a gift.
Use it!

-Shawntel D. Carey, 2011

---◆---

Love, Truth & Accountability

---◆---

Disconnect from those that
do not value you while continuing
to show appreciation to those who do.

-Shawntel D. Carey, 2021

When you realize that you've outgrown
your current network, start, at that moment,
to build a new one. Leave the unimaginative
and unsupportive where they stand.

-Shawntel D. Carey, 2021

Remember the people who supported you
during the good and bad times.
Those people are keepers!

-Shawntel D. Carey, 2021

Never be okay with a person who is okay with watching you struggle. People in your life should be protectors, providers, and partners.

-Shawntel D. Carey, 2020

Give your love to the one
that always chooses you
over everything and everyone.

-Shawntel D. Carey, 2022

You deserve love because you are lovable.
You know how to give love in return.
Therefore, you should not accept anything
less than wholehearted true love.

-Shawntel D. Carey, 2020

If that person doesn't stand for the truth
nor accept accountability for their actions,
then you don't need them in your life.

-Shawntel D. Carey, 2020

Ladies, never date a man that'll watch you struggle,
I urge you to remain single and resourceful
especially, if such a gentleman is an option.

-Shawntel D. Carey, 2022

Be interested in getting to know
as many decent people as you possibly can.
Such a process is slow because time is the main element.

-Shawntel D. Carey, 2021

Temporary people may turn
into permanent consequences.

Shawntel D. Carey, 2022

Believe in love.

-Shawntel D. Carey, 2021

Seek and offer discipline, integrity, honesty, courage, loyalty, fortitude, consistency, respect and stability, no matter the nature of the relationship. Be a good person to whomever you encounter.

-Shawntel D. Carey, 2021

Restoration & Resilience

Prayer works.
Let us pray for everyone.

-Shawntel D. Carey, 2020

At times there is nothing but uncertainty
surrounding us, but if we trust and
have faith, our path will be guided.

-Shawntel D. Carey, 2011

We often wonder why some things end the way they do, yet it's useless to dwell on it; everything has its own lifecycle.

-Shawntel D. Carey, 2011

I believe!
I believe!
I dare to believe in miracles.

-Shawntel D. Carey, 2018

Focus on the future, not the past.
Give yourself time to adjust while
being eager to find out what comes next.

-Shawntel D. Carey, 2011

I believe everyone should
at some point in their
lives seek counseling.

- Shawntel D. Carey, 2019

I am a proponent of therapy
as well as a beneficiary.

- Shawntel D. Carey, 2019

Grateful for those who are solid in
my presence as well as behind my back.

-Shawntel D. Carey, 2021

You are a good person and
good shall come to you.

-Shawntel D. Carey, 2020

Faith to Fruition.
Repeat until complete.
Anything worthwhile will not come easy,
no matter who you are.

-Shawntel D. Carey, 2018

When life gets too heavy to handle,
duck down and remain still until you
have definitively decided your next move.

-Shawntel D. Carey, 2019

Everything and everyone
has an expiration date.
Know this!

-Shawntel D. Carey, 2021

Today, I woke up inspired by
the past, present and future.

-Shawntel D. Carey, 2021

——— ✦ ———

Becoming Your Highest Self

——— ✦ ———

Understand your circumstances
as they come and go. Set goals.
Know where you're going and
how to get there. Map it out.
Let nothing stop you.

-Shawntel D. Carey, 2007

Wanna make money?
Then work at the mint.
Wanna earn money? Then set goals,
use your mind, work, and act!

-Shawntel D. Carey, 2010

Sometimes you just have to celebrate yourself,
so today look in the mirror and say,
"I knew you could do it!"

-Shawntel D. Carey, 2020

If someone wants something bad enough,
that person will do whatever it takes to get it.

-Shawntel D. Carey, 2020

You can change your life...
if you purposefully change your thoughts.

-Shawntel D. Carey, 2019

Be Courageous. Be Original.

-Shawntel D. Carey, 2018

Inspire, Motivate and Elevate.
Simply just my life's passion.

-Shawntel D. Carey, 2019

You have already proven that you can handle this life alone. You got this! However, it would be nice to have somebody that has your back.

-Shawntel D. Carey, 2019

You Can and You Will!
Let Nothing Stop You!

-Shawntel D. Carey, 2020

When one seems to have no choice
(at least in their own mind) moving
forward becomes inevitable.

-Shawntel D. Carey, 2018

I love helping people realize their purpose in life.
It is such a blessing to be an inspiration to others.
I love to inspire and motivate others.
I live to inspire through my testimony.

-Shawntel D. Carey, 2019

The appropriate actions will follow
once you have made up your mind
and have committed to the process.
Define your process in five steps or less...
You got this!

-Shawntel D. Carey, 2019

Once your mindset and priorities have changed,
there will come a time when you must
take stock and realize that material items
mean nothing more than
souvenirs of past achievements.

-Shawntel D. Carey, 2021

———— ✦ ————

Citizenship & Responsibility

 ———— ✦ ————

I'm a nerd and actually enjoy reading
The Constitution of the United States of America
every household should have one.

-Shawntel D. Carey, 2020

Be Powerfully Organized.
Create the pathway.

-Shawntel D. Carey, 2021

Elect government officials that will improve your life
via the policies and laws they implement.
YOUR VOTE IS IMPORTANT!

-Shawntel D. Carey, 2018

It's important to vote in
Local, State and Federal Elections.

-Shawntel D. Carey, 2018

Paying taxes and voting are civic duties.
One is optional and the other is not.

-Shawntel D. Carey, 2020

Researching and selecting the appropriate
political candidates is one of our
greatest voluntary civic responsibilities as
a citizen of the United States of America.

-Shawntel D. Carey, 2020

My wish is for the average citizen to become
obsessed with setting political agendas
via the public policy formation process.

-Shawntel D. Carey, 2019

I am overwhelmingly fascinated by
the alliance between
private power and public purpose.

-Shawntel D. Carey, 2022

Conspicuous Consumption
and Materialistic Consumerism
is of no interest.

-Shawntel D. Carey, 2022

Principles to Live By

The day is upon us;
let us make the best of it.

-Shawntel D. Carey, 2025

She's different. Burn Rubber.

-Shawntel D. Carey, 2021

Happiness is as simple as fresh flowers.

-Shawntel D. Carey, 2020

Honor your words with your actions,
therefore, those who you choose to
be in your life must do the same.

-Shawntel D. Carey, 2021

New Money is SO LOUD!

-Shawntel D. Carey, 2019

Go on Vacation, Drink Gin, and be Silly.

-Shawntel D. Carey, 2019

Two of my favorite things:
Books and Diamonds.

-Shawntel D. Carey, 2021

Who's thinking about dating or
being in a relationship? Not me!
Let's start a business and earn money.

-Shawntel D. Carey, 2021

No matter where you are,
or what you are doing,
do your best and be the best.

-Shawntel D. Carey, 2019

I am a different kind of lady.
I collect books.
I appreciate original prints
and first editions.

-Shawntel D. Carey, 2000

If you find yourself ready to give up,
pull back and remember
my favorite quote by Winston Churchill
"Success is going from failure to failure
without losing enthusiasm."

-Shawntel D. Carey, 2020

Strive to be authentic. Be real.
By all means, just be yourself.

-Shawntel D. Carey, 2019

When you know you deserve more,
or simply just feel that you need more,
always choose you!
Do not allow yourself to be undervalued.

-Shawntel D. Carey, 2020

I try extremely hard not to use the words dumb or stupid when referring to others, but some people leave us with no choice.

-Shawntel D. Carey, 2018

I'm rooting for you!
Love seeing you win.
Keep Winning!

-Shawntel D. Carey, 2019

Test people early, then quickly remove those who
do not have your best interest at heart
from your life, but don't burn bridges.
Those that remain will always be there,
no matter the time, space, or circumstance.
Know the difference.

-Shawntel D. Carey, 2017

Take only the real ones
with you on the journey ahead.
Good Luck with that!

-Shawntel D. Carey, 2019

To anyone out there struggling
academically or as a practitioner, I say,
"Hang in there; it gets easier, at least,
this is what I continuously tell myself."

-Shawntel D. Carey, 2021

There was a man that I once heard say,
"Pay Me or Pay Me No Attention."

-Shawntel D. Carey, 2019

I got a dress to wear, so I'll be there...

-Shawntel D. Carey, 2020

Value peace more than anything;
be authentically happy.

-Shawntel D. Carey, 2022

Everything in life runs its course.
The impasse is where final decisions are made.

-Shawntel D. Carey, 2019

Life is a perpetual state of
contemplation and decision-making.

-Shawntel D. Carey, 2020

STAY CONNECTED

We'd love to hear from you.

Email: sdccompasspublishingllc@gmail.com

For updates, new releases, and merchandise:
- **LinkedIn:** SDC Compass Publishing LLC
- **Instagram:** @SDCCompassPublishing
- **Facebook:** SDC Compass Publishing

Share your favorite quotes and tag us: **#QuotesBySDC**

SDC Compass Publishing LLC

Purpose-Driven Publishing, Community Focused.